REPORTING RULES FOR WIDELY HELD FIXED INVESTMENT TRUSTS (US INTERNAL REVENUE SERVICE REGULATION) (IRS) (2018 EDITION)

Updated as of May 29, 2018

THE LAW LIBRARY

TABLE OF CONTENTS

AGENCY	4
ACTION	4
SUMMARY	4
DATES	4
FOR FURTHER INFORMATION CONTACT	4
SUPPLEMENTARY INFORMATION	4
Paperwork Reduction Act	5
Background	5
Summary of Comments and Explanation of Revisions	6
I. Application of the WHFIT Reporting Rules to NMWHFITs	6
II. Applicability of the WHFIT Reporting Rules to WHMTs	11
III. Requirement to Register and Continued Consideration of a WHFIT Directory	13
IV. Form 1041 Reporting	14
Effective Date	14
Special Analyses	14
Drafting Information	15
LIST OF SUBJECTS IN 26 CFR PART 1	15
REGULATORY TEXT	15
PART 1 INCOME TAXES	15
Authority:	15
§ 1.671-5 Reporting for widely held fixed investment trusts.	16
§ 1.671-5T [Removed]	29

AGENCY

Internal Revenue Service (IRS), Treasury.

ACTION

Final regulations and removal of the temporary regulations.

SUMMARY

This document contains final regulations amending § 1.671-5 which provides reporting rules for widely held fixed investment trusts (WHFITs). These final regulations clarify and simplify reporting for trustees and middlemen of non-mortgage widely held fixed investment trusts (NMWHFITs). These final regulations also provide temporary safe harbor reporting rules for widely held mortgage trusts (WHMTs) that are outside the WHMT safe harbor. The preamble to these regulations also provides that trustees of WHFITs are to indicate on the Form 1041, "U.S. Income Tax Return for Estates and Trusts," filed for a WHFIT's 2006 calendar year that the return is a final return.

DATES

Effective Date: These regulations are effective December 29, 2006.

Applicability Date: For date of applicability see § 1.671-5(n).

FOR FURTHER INFORMATION CONTACT

Faith Colson, (202) 622-3060 (not a toll-free number).

SUPPLEMENTARY INFORMATION

Paperwork Reduction Act

The collection of information contained in these final regulations has been previously reviewed and approved by the Office of Management and Budget in accordance with the Paperwork Reduction Act of 1995 (44 U.S.C. 3507) under control number 1545-1540. The collection of information in these final regulations is in § 1.671-5. This information is required to be reported to beneficial owners of trust interests to enable them to correctly report their share of the items of income, deduction, and credit of the WHFIT in which they have invested. This information is also required to be reported to the IRS to enable the IRS to verify that trustees and middlemen are accurately reporting information to beneficial owners of trust interests and that beneficial owners are properly reporting their ownership of a trust interest.

An agency may not conduct or sponsor, and a person is not required to respond to, a collection of information unless it displays a valid control number.

The estimated annual burden per recordkeeper varies from 1 to 4 hours, depending on individual circumstances, with an estimated average of 2 hours. Comments concerning the accuracy of this burden estimate should be sent to the Internal Revenue Service, Attn: IRS Reports Clearance Officer, SE:W:CAR:MP:T:T:SP, Washington DC 20224, and to the Office of Management and Budget, Attn: Desk Officer for the Department of Treasury, Office of Information and Regulatory Affairs, Washington, DC 20503.

Books or records relating to a collection of information must be retained as long as their contents might become material in the administration of any internal revenue law. Generally, tax returns and tax return information are confidential, as required by 26 U.S.C. 6103.

Background

This document contains amendments to 26 CFR part 1. On January 24, 2006, the Internal Revenue Service (IRS) and the Treasury Department published the WHFIT reporting rules in the Federal Register (TD 9241) (71 FR 4002) under § 1.671-5 (WHFIT reporting rules). On August 3, 2006, in response to comments received subsequent to the publication of the WHFIT reporting rules, the IRS and the Treasury Department published final and temporary regulations (TD 9279) (71 FR 43968) (temporary regulations) as well as proposed regulations that, in part, cross-referenced the temporary regulations (71 FR 43998) (proposed regulations) (REG-125071-06) in the Federal Register. No public hearing was requested or held with respect to the temporary or proposed regulations. Written comments responding to those regulations were received. After consideration of the comments, the proposed regulations, with certain revisions, are adopted as final regulations by this Treasury decision, and the corresponding temporary regulations are removed. The comments and the revisions are discussed in this preamble.

Summary of Comments and Explanation of Revisions

I. Application of the WHFIT Reporting Rules to NMWHFITs

A. The Qualified NMWHFIT Exception

Trustees and middlemen of NMWHFITs that satisfy the qualified NMWHFIT exception in § 1.671-5(c)(2)(iv)(E) are excepted from reporting information regarding market discount and bond premium, and are permitted to use the simplified reporting for sales and dispositions of trust assets in § 1.671-5(c)(2)(iv)(B) and the simplified reporting rules for sales or redemptions of trust interests in § 1.671-5(c)(2)(v)(C). The temporary regulations provide that the qualified NMWHFIT exception is satisfied if the calendar year for which the trustee is reporting begins before January 1, 2011, and the NMWHFIT meets any of the following requirements: (1) the NMWHFIT has a start-up date as defined in § 1.671-5(b)(19) before February 23, 2006; (2) the registration statement for the NMWHFIT becomes effective under the Securities Act of 1933, as amended (15 U.S.C. 77a, et. seq.) (Securities Act of 1933) and trust interests are offered for sale to the public before February 23, 2006; or (3) the registration statement of the NMWHFIT becomes effective under the Securities Act of 1933 and trust interests are offered for sale to the public on or after February 23, 2006 and before July 31, 2006, and the NMWHFIT is fully funded before October 1, 2006. These final regulations retain this amendment to the WHFIT reporting rules. Additionally, commentators on the temporary regulations expressed concern that certain trusts that otherwise satisfy the eligibility requirements for the qualified NMWHFIT exception would be disqualified because additional assets are deposited into the trust pursuant to a distribution reinvestment program. These final regulations clarify that for the purpose of determining whether a NMWHFIT is fully funded before October 1, 2006, deposits to the NMWHFIT pursuant to a distribution reinvestment program that is consistent with the requirements of § 301.7701-4(c) will be disregarded.

Commentators have also expressed concern regarding NMWHFITs that hold debt instruments (fixed income trusts) that were originated before the WHFIT reporting rules were published in the Federal Register. Commentators are concerned because the simplified reporting permitted under the exception terminates after December 31, 2010, and many fixed income trusts will be unable to comply with the WHFIT reporting rules once the simplified reporting permitted under the qualified NMWHFIT exception terminates because these NMWHFITs generally are not able to engage in pro-rata sales of trust assets to effect redemptions. Commentators have requested that these NMWHFITs be permanently permitted to report consistent with the qualified NMWHFIT exception. In response, these regulations amend § 1.671-5(c)(2)(iv)(E) to eliminate the requirement that the trustee must be reporting for a year that begins before January 1,

2011 for the NMWHFIT to be eligible for the simplified reporting. Accordingly, NMWHFITs that satisfy the qualified NMWHFIT exception and continue in existence after December 31, 2010 may report under the simplified reporting permitted under the exception until those NMWHFITs terminate.

B. Simplified Reporting of Sales and Redemptions of Trust Interests

With respect to the sale or redemption of a trust interest, section 1.671-5(c)(2)(v) of the WHFIT reporting rules requires trustees and middlemen to provide information regarding the sales assets proceeds (as defined in § 1.671-5(b)(17)) or the redemption assets proceeds (as defined in § 1.671-5(b)(14)) as well as the income that is attributable to a redeeming, selling or purchasing beneficial owner up to the date of the sale or redemption of a trust interest. Section 1.671-5(c)(2)(v)(C) excepts a NMWHFIT from the requirement to provide information to enable requesting persons to differentiate between income and proceeds if substantially all the NMWHFIT's income is comprised of dividends (equity trusts) and the NMWHFIT is required by its governing document to distribute the cash held for distribution by the NMWHFIT at least monthly. The temporary regulations, and these final regulations revise § 1.671-5(c)(2)(v)(C) to provide that a NMWHFIT will be considered to have satisfied the requirement that it distribute the cash held for distribution monthly notwithstanding the fact that, although the governing document requires monthly distributions, the governing document of the NMWHFIT also permits the trustee to forego making its normally required monthly distribution if the cash held for distribution is less than 0.1 percent of the net asset value of the trust (aggregate fair market value of the trust's assets less the trust's liabilities) as of the date that the amount of the monthly distribution is required to be determined.

Commentators have indicated that it will be extremely difficult for a certain class of NMWHFITs that are not equity trusts to comply with § 1.671-5(c)(2)(v). These NMWHFITs hold assets that produce income that is treated as interest income, not dividend income, for Federal income tax purposes. The assets of these NMWHFITs, however, are similar to assets that produce dividend income in that the assets are traded on a recognized exchange or securities market in such a way that the price of the assets is determined without a component attributable to accrued interest. As with NMWHFITs that hold assets that produce dividend income, it is difficult for the trustees and middlemen of these NMWHFITs to determine the income attributable to a redeeming, selling, or purchasing beneficial owner between trust distribution dates. For these reasons, the final regulations provide that NMWHFITs that hold assets that produce income that is treated as interest income for Federal income tax purposes will also qualify for the simplified reporting under § 1.671-5(c)(2)(v)(C) but only if the assets are traded on a recognized exchange or securities market in such a way that the price of the assets is determined without a component attributable to accrued interest.

C. Simplified Reporting for Sales and Dispositions by Certain NMWHFITs

In addition to the qualified NMWHFIT exception, the WHFIT reporting rules provide that the trustees of NMWHFITs that meet the general de minimis test in § 1.671-5(c)(2)(iv)(D)(1) are only required, under § 1.671-5(c)(2)(iv)(B), to provide information regarding the amount of trust sales proceeds distributed to a beneficial owner. A NMWHFIT meets the general de minimis test if trust sales proceeds (as defined in § 1.671-5(b)(21)) for the calendar year are not more than five percent of the net asset value of the trust as of the later of January 1 of the year for which the trustee is reporting or the start-up date. The reason for the de minimis exception, as stated in the preamble to the WHFIT reporting rules, is that the IRS and the Treasury Department believe that if a NMWHFIT only sells or disposes of assets infrequently, although there may be some deferral of gains and losses if sales and dispositions are not fully reported, the deferral is acceptable, in light of the burden of fully, accurately reporting the sales and dispositions.

Commentators on the WHFIT reporting rules reported that trustees of NMWHFITs frequently have to sell trust assets to obtain cash to effect redemptions and that, because of those sales, many NMWHFITs will not be able to meet the general de minimis test in § 1.671-5(c)(2)(iv)(D)(1). Commentators on the WHFIT reporting rules requested that those regulations be amended to provide for reduced reporting where this will have little or no compliance impact. In response to those comments, the temporary regulations provide a number of modifications to the NMWHFIT reporting rules as applied to certain sales and dispositions of trust assets by NMWHFITs. Those modifications, as well as additional modification made by these final regulations, include:

1. NMWHFIT Final Calendar Year Exception

Section 1.671-5T(c)(2)(iv)(F) of the temporary regulations provides that all NMWHFITs qualify for the simplified reporting in § 1.671-5T(c)(2)(iv)(B) in the final calendar year of the NMWHFIT, regardless of whether the NMWHFIT has otherwise satisfied the general de minimis test, provided that a beneficial owner cannot roll over its investment in the NMWHFIT to another WHFIT. Commentators on the temporary regulations requested that the IRS and Treasury Department clarify that a taxable roll-over would not preclude a trustee from reporting under the final year exception. Accordingly, these regulations remove the reference to a roll-over and instead require that, to be eligible for the final year exception, beneficial owners of trust interests must exchange their trust interests for cash or be treated as having exchanged their trust interests for cash for Federal income tax purposes upon the termination of the trust.

2. Pro-rata Sales to Effect Redemptions Exception

Section 1.671-5T(c)(2)(iv)(G) of the temporary regulations provides that a pro-rata sale of a trust asset to effect a redemption is not required to be reported under § 1.671-5. The temporary regulations describe a pro-rata sale of a trust asset as occurring when (1) a trust interest holder tenders one or more trust interests for redemption; (2) the trustee sells the pro-rata share of a trust asset that is deemed to be owned by the trust interest holder as a result of the trust interest holder's ownership of the trust interest or interests tendered for redemption; (3) the trustee engages in the sale solely to obtain cash that is immediately distributed to the redeeming trust interest holder as a result of the redemption; and (4) the redemption is reported as required under § 1.671-5(c)(2)(v).

Commentators on the temporary regulations have requested that the pro-rata sales to effect a redemption exception in the temporary regulations be adjusted to accommodate economic and practical issues that trustees confront in executing sales of trust assets to effect redemptions. These commentators requested that the pro-rata sales to effect a redemption exception be revised to provide the trustee with some flexibility regarding the time period in which the trustee has to execute sales following the tender of trust interests for redemptions and to permit trustees to aggregate sales of assets from several redemptions for the purpose of testing whether the asset sales have been pro-rata. In response, the final regulations provide that pro-rata sales to effect redemptions occur when (i) one or more trust interests are tendered for redemption; (ii) the trustee identifies the pro-rata share of the trust assets deemed to be owned by the trust interest or interests tendered for redemption, and sells those assets as soon as practicable; (iii) proceeds from the sale of the identified assets are used solely to effect redemptions; and (iv) the redemptions are reported as required under § 1.671-5(c)(2)(v) by the trustee.

Additionally, the final regulations provide that the trustee may compare the aggregate of the pro-rata share of the trust assets deemed to be owned by the trust interests tendered for redemption and the sales of assets sold to effect redemptions determine the pro-rata sales of assets to effect redemptions for a calendar month. Further, if the aggregate pro-rata share of the assets deemed to be owned by the redeemed trust interests for the month equals a fractional share, the trustee may round that amount to the next whole share for the purpose of determining the pro-rata sales to effect a redemption for the calendar month.

3. De minimis Test Modifications

Section 1.671-5T(b)(21) of the temporary regulations provides an amended definition of trust sales proceeds that excludes the gross proceeds paid to a NMWHFIT for a pro-rata sale of a trust asset to effect a redemption. The effect of this change in the definition of trust sales proceeds is to exclude the proceeds from pro-rata sales of trust assets to effect redemptions when determining whether a trust has met the general de minimis test. Since only the proceeds from non pro-rata sales of trust assets are considered for purposes of determining whether a NMWHFIT meets the general de minimis test, more trusts will meet the general de minimis test and qualify for the reduced reporting in § 1.671-5(c)(2)(iv)(B). This amended definition is adopted by these final regulations.

Commentators on the temporary regulations requested that the final regulations also except certain other trust sales proceeds for the purpose of determining whether a NMWHFIT has met the general de minimis test if these sales are fully reported under § 1.671-5(c)(2)(iv)(A) (the general reporting rules for sales and dispositions). These sales and dispositions include corporate reorganizations and restructurings for which the trust receives cash, the sale of securities received by the trust in corporate reorganizations and restructurings (including conversions of closed-end investment companies to open-end investment companies), principal prepayments, bond calls, bond maturities, and the sale of securities by the trustee as required by the governing document or applicable law governing fiduciaries in order to maintain the sound investment character of the trust, and any other nonvolitional dispositions.

The IRS and the Treasury Department agree that this exclusion may be appropriate but are concerned that there may be some potential for abuse if trustees can choose to fully report some of these sales and not fully report other sales. Accordingly, the final regulations provide that the trust sales proceeds from these sales and dispositions may be excluded when determining whether the general de minimis test has been met, provided that the trustee consistently reports all such sales or dispositions, other than certain small excepted sales or dispositions (described in § 1.671-5(c)(2)(iv)(D)(4)(iii)), under § 1.671-5(c)(2)(iv)(A) during the life of the WHFIT.

The regulations currently provide that a WHFIT meets the general de minimis test in § 1.671-5(c)(2)(iv)(D)(1) for its initial year if trust sales proceeds equal five percent or less of the net fair market value of the trust assets as of the start-up date. The start-up date is defined as the date when substantially all of the assets have been deposited with the trustee. Commentators suggested that the regulations provide trustees with an alternative date for measuring whether the de minimis test has been met for the initial trust year. They suggested that trustees be permitted to measure whether the de minimis test has been met by using the net fair market value of the trust's assets as of the date of the last deposit of trust assets into the NMWHFIT (not including any deposit of assets into the NMWHFIT pursuant to a distribution reinvestment program), not to exceed 90 days after the date the registration statement of the WHFIT becomes effective under the Securities Act of 1933. The final regulations adopt this suggestion.

The special WHMT de minimis test in § 1.671-5(c)(2)(iv)(D)(2) of the WHFIT reporting rules was added to the WHFIT reporting rules in response to comments from the WHMT industry indicating that WHMT trustees would have difficulty applying the general de minimis test because it would be extremely difficult for the trustee to determine the fair market value of the mortgages held by the WHMT on an annual basis, as required under the general de minimis test. Under the special WHMT de minimis test, trustees of certain WHMTs are permitted to determine whether the de minimis test has been met using the outstanding principal balance of the mortgages of the trust as of January 1 rather than the net fair market value of the trust's assets. A commentator suggested that this de minimis test be expanded so that all WHFITs with hard to value debt instruments be permitted to use this de minimis test. In response, the IRS and Treasury Department request that trustees of WHFITs that hold hard to value debt instruments and that believe the application of the WHMT de minimis test to the instruments held by the WHFIT for which the trustees act would be useful, submit additional comments on this issue. The final regulations amend § 1.671-5(c)(2)(iv)(D)(2) to provide that the application of the special de minimis test may be expanded by revenue ruling or other published guidance.

4. Non Taxable Exchanges of Assets

Commentators suggested that the final regulations provide an exception to the reporting rules for sales and dispositions of trust assets for exchanges of trust assets that result from nontaxable corporate reorganizations. The final regulations adopt this suggestion.

D. Market Discount

Commentators requested amendments to the information required to be reported under the NMWHFIT safe harbor with respect to market discount. If a NMWHFIT is required to provide information regarding market discount under the general rules in § 1.671-5(c)(2)(vii), the NMWHFIT safe harbor provides that a trustee's requirement to provide information regarding market discount is satisfied by providing information regarding the portion of the trust that the assets sold represented. Assuming that a trust interest holder purchased its interest at a discount, it was contemplated that the trust interest holder would allocate the same portion of its discount to the sale as the assets represented to the NMWHFIT.

This information was incomplete, however, with respect to a NMWHFIT holding debt instruments with original issue discount (OID). Under both the general provisions (§ 1.671-5(c)(2)(ii)(A) and (vii)) and the safe harbor (§ 1.671-5(f)(1)(vii) and (viii)), OID information and market discount information are required to be calculated and provided separately. Accordingly, for beneficial owners to determine the amount of market discount an owner must allocate to a particular sale or disposition of a debt instrument by the NMWHFIT, § 1.671-5(f)(1)(viii)(A) is amended with respect to NMWHFITs that hold debt instruments with OID, to include a requirement that trustees provide a list of the aggregate adjusted issue prices of the debt instruments held by the NMWHFIT per trust interest as of the start-up date or the measuring date (as defined in § 1.671-5(c)(2)(iv)(D)(1)) whichever will provide the more accurate information, as well as of January 1 of each subsequent year of the NMWHFIT. The IRS and the Treasury Department expect that beneficial owners of trust interests will use the adjusted issue price for the trust's debt instruments per trust interest for the year in which the beneficial owner purchased its interest to determine whether a trust interest has market discount.

II. Applicability of the WHFIT Reporting Rules to WHMTs

A. Temporary WHMT Safe Harbor for WHMTs That Hold Interests in a REMIC, Hold Interests in Another WHFIT, or Hold or Issue Stripped Interests

The WHFIT reporting rules include a safe harbor for WHMTs that directly hold mortgages (as defined in § 1.671-5(b)(11)) and issue trust interests that represent an equal pro-rata right to payments of interest and principal on the underlying mortgages. WHMTs that hold or issue stripped interests, hold interests in another WHFIT, or hold interests in a REMIC, are not eligible to report under the WHMT safe harbor. The IRS and the Treasury Department received comments expressing concern about the application of the WHFIT reporting rules to WHMTs that are outside the WHMT safe harbor because trustees and middlemen of these WHMTs are required to comply with the general WHFIT reporting rules in § 1.671-5(c). The commentators contended that some of the information required to be reported under the general information rules would be burdensome to obtain and moreover, is not required by beneficial owners to accurately report the tax consequences of owning a trust interest. In response to these concerns, pending the issuance of additional WHMT safe harbors, these final regulations provide a temporary safe harbor for all WHMTs that are outside the WHMT safe harbor in § 1.671-5(g) of the WHFIT reporting rules because they hold or issue stripped interests, hold interests in a REMIC or hold an interest in another WHMT. Under the safe harbor, a trustee will be deemed to satisfy the requirements of § 1.671-5(c)(1) if the trustee calculates and provides trust information in a manner that enables a requesting person to provide trust information to a beneficial owner of a trust interest that enables the owner to reasonably accurately report the tax consequences of its ownership of a trust interest on the Federal income tax return of the beneficial owner.

Additionally, in order to be deemed to have satisfied the requirements of § 1.671-5(c)(1), the trustee must provide information regarding market discount and original issue discount (OID) that is calculated in any reasonable manner consistent with section 1272(a)(6). Pending the issuance of additional guidance, it is intended that this safe harbor except trustees from any penalties that may apply for not fully complying with paragraph (c) of the WHFIT reporting rules where it can be shown that full compliance with paragraph (c) is unnecessary in order to provide trust interest holders with appropriate information. A trustee or middleman required to provide information to the IRS under § 1.671-5(d) and to beneficial owners under paragraph § 1.671-5(e) may satisfy those obligations by calculating and providing trust information consistent with the information provided by the trustee under this safe harbor.

B. Application of the Requirement To Provide Market Discount and OID Information for Existing WHMTs

Section 1.671-5(c)(2)(ii)(A) requires a trustee of a WHFIT to provide information regarding OID. Commentators have expressed concern regarding the application of this requirement to existing WHMTs because the historical information that would enable the trustee to provide OID information has never been provided or maintained by the trustee or the persons responsible for information reporting. Commentators contend that it is unlikely that these trustees will be able to comply with this requirement for existing WHMTs. The IRS and the Treasury Department recognize that, in some cases, the information necessary for a WHMT to comply with this provision may not be available. If it can be demonstrated that a trustee of a WHMT with a start-up date on or after August 13, 1998 and on or before January 24, 2006, has attempted in good faith, but without success, to obtain the historical information required to provide OID information, the IRS will not impose any penalties that would apply under § 1.671-5(l) of the WHFIT reporting rules (redesignated § 1.671-5(m) by these final regulations) as a result of a trustee's failure to comply with the requirement to provide OID information. Further, § 1.671-5(c)(2)(ii)(A) of these final regulations excepts a trustee of a WHMT with a start-up date prior to August 13, 1998 from the requirement to provide OID information. For purposes of calculating the market discount fraction under the WHMT safe harbor in § 1.671-5(g)(1)(v), these trustees may assume that the WHMT is holding mortgages that were issued without OID.

The WHMT safe harbor provisions for calculating OID information in § 1.671-5(g)(i)(iv) and market discount information in § 1.671-5(g)(1)(v) require trustees to use the prepayment assumption used in pricing the original issue of trust interests. Commentators have indicated that trustees of existing WHMTs may not know the prepayment assumption used in pricing the original issue of trust interests. In response, the safe harbor is amended to provide that if the trustee does not know the prepayment assumption used in pricing the original issue of trust interests for a WHMT with a start-up date prior to January 24, 2006, and the trustee makes a good faith effort without success to obtain the prepayment assumption, the trustee may use any reasonable prepayment assumption when calculating OID and market discount information for that WHMT.

III. Requirement to Register and Continued Consideration of a WHFIT Directory

Prior to the publication of the WHFIT reporting rules, commentators expressed concern that middlemen would not be able to identify a client's investment as an investment in a WHFIT and suggested that the IRS publish a directory or list of WHFITs that would include the name and CUSIP number of each WHFIT, along with the name, address and telephone number of the WHFIT's representative. Commentators noted that a publicly available directory or list would assist middlemen and brokers in identifying a client's investment as an investment in a WHFIT and in locating the WHFIT's representative. The WHFIT reporting rules did not provide for a directory and instead, required the trustee to identify a representative of the trust to provide trust information in a publication generally read by and available to requesting persons, in the trust's prospectus, or on the trustee's Internet Web site.

Following the publication of the WHFIT reporting rules, additional comments were received regarding the need for a directory of WHFITs. In response to those comments, the proposed regulations indicated that the IRS and Treasury Department considered expanding Publication 938, "Real Estate Mortgage Investment Conduits (REMICs) Reporting Information (and other Collateralized Debt Obligations (CDOs))," or creating a separate publication to list WHMT trustees and NMWHFITs. The IRS and Treasury Department continue to consider how a directory of WHFITs could be implemented. Pending the publication of such a directory, trustees must provide information regarding a trust representative in the manner provided in the WHFIT reporting rules.

IV. Form 1041 Reporting

A trustee of a WHFIT must indicate on the Form 1041 filed for the 2006 calendar year that the return is a final return.

Effective Date

These final amendments are effective December 29, 2006. In general, these final regulations are applicable to the reporting required under § 1.671-5 as of January 1, 2007 (see § 1.671-5(m) (redesignated § 1.671-5(n) by these final regulations)) and will be applied as though these amendments were included in the WHFIT reporting rules. The IRS and the Treasury Department are aware that some trustees and middlemen were unable to complete updates to their computer and information reporting systems to comply with the WHFIT reporting rules until the amendments to the WHFIT reporting rules included in these regulations are finalized. Accordingly, the IRS will not impose any penalties that would apply under § 1.671-5(l) (redesignated § 1.671-5(m) by these final regulations) of the WHFIT reporting rules as a result of the failure to comply with the WHFIT reporting rules as amended by these final regulations with respect to the 2007 calendar year in cases where a trustee or middleman was unable to change its information reporting systems to comply with the WHFIT reporting rules because of uncertainty regarding the application of certain provisions of those rules pending the publication of these final regulations. For example, penalties will not be imposed on a trustee of a NMWHFIT that reports the amount of trust sales proceeds distributed to trust interest holders for the 2007 calendar year under § 1.671-5(c)(2)(iv)(B) even though the trustee is unable to determine whether the NMWHFIT has met the de minimis test for the 2007 calendar year, provided that the trustee's failure to determine whether a NMWHFIT has met the de minimis test results from the trustee's inability to alter its existing information reporting systems by January 1, 2007, to capture the necessary information. As an additional example, penalties will not be imposed on the trustees or the middlemen of WHMTs that are unable to comply with certain provisions of the WHFIT reporting rules with respect to the 2007 calendar year because those trustees and middlemen were not able to change their existing reporting systems to comply with the WHFIT reporting rules pending the publication of these final regulations.

Special Analyses

It has been determined that these final regulations are not a significant regulatory action as defined in Executive Order 12866. Therefore, a regulatory assessment is not required. It is hereby certified that this regulation will not have a significant economic impact on a substantial number of small entities. This certification is based on the fact that the regulations will not have a significant economic impact on small entities because the reporting burdens in these regulations will fall primarily on large brokerage firms, large banks, and other large entities acting as trustees or middlemen, most of which are not small entities within the meaning of the Regulatory Flexibility Act (5 U.S.C. chapter 6). Thus, a substantial number of small entities are not expected to be affected. Therefore, a Regulatory Flexibility Analysis under the Regulatory Flexibility Act (5 U.S.C. chapter 6) is not required. Pursuant to section 7805(f) of the Internal Revenue Code, the notice of proposed rulemaking preceding this regulation was submitted to the Chief Counsel for Advocacy of the Small Business Administration for comment on its impact on small business.

Drafting Information

The principal author of these regulations is Faith Colson, Office of Associate Chief Counsel (Passthroughs & Special Industries). However, other personnel from the IRS and the Treasury Department participated in their development.

LIST OF SUBJECTS IN 26 CFR PART 1

Income taxes, Reporting and recordkeeping requirements.

REGULATORY TEXT

Adoption of Amendments to the Regulations

Accordingly, 26 CFR part 1 is amended as follows:

PART 1 INCOME TAXES

Paragraph 1. The authority citation for part 1 continues to read, in part, as follows:

Authority:

26 U.S.C. 7805 * * *

Par. 2. Section 1.671-5 is amended by:

1. Revising paragraph (a) by redesignating entries for paragraphs (h), (j), (k), (l), and (m) as entries for paragraphs (j), (k), (l), (m) and (n) and adding a new entry for paragraph (h).

2. Revising paragraphs (b)(5), (b)(8), (b)(21), (c)(2)(ii)(A), (c)(2)(iv), (c)(2)(v), (c)(2)(vi), (c)(2)(vii), (d)(2)(ii)(C), (d)(2)(ii)(F), (d)(2)(ii)(G), (f)(1), (f)(1)(i)(A), (f)(1)(viii)(A), (f)(2)(viii)(A), (f)(3)(i)(A)(1), (f)(3)(i)(B)(5), (f)(3)(i)(B)(9), (f)(3)(ii)(B)(4)(i), (f)(3)(ii)(B)(5), (f)(3)(ii)(B)(6), (g)(1)(iv)(A)(2), and (g)(1)(v)(A).

3. Redesignating paragraphs (h), (j), (k), (l) and (m) as (j), (k), (l), (m) and (n) respectively.

4. Adding new paragraph (h).

Revising newly designated paragraph (m).

The additions and revisions read as follows:

§ 1.671-5 Reporting for widely held fixed investment trusts.

(a) * * *

(h) Additional safe harbors.

(1) Temporary safe harbors.

(2) Additional safe harbors provided by other published guidance.

* * * * *

(b) * * *

(5) The cash held for distribution is the amount of cash held by the WHFIT (other than trust sales proceeds and proceeds from sales described in paragraphs (c)(2)(iv)(D)(4), (G), and (H) of this section) less reasonably required reserve funds as of the date that the amount of a distribution is required to be determined under the WHFIT's governing document.

* * * * *

(8) An in-kind redemption is a redemption in which a beneficial owner receives a pro-rata share of each of the assets of the WHFIT that the beneficial owner is deemed to own

under section 671. For example, for purposes of this paragraph (b)(8), if beneficial owner A owns a one percent interest in a WHFIT that holds 100 shares of X corporation stock, so that A is considered to own a one percent interest in each of the 100 shares, A's pro-rata share of the X corporation stock for this purpose is one share of X corporation stock.

* * * * *

(21) Trust sales proceeds equal the amount paid to a WHFIT for the sale or disposition of an asset held by the WHFIT, including principal payments received by the WHFIT that completely retire a debt instrument (other than a final scheduled principal payment) and pro-rata partial principal prepayments described under § 1.1275-2(f)(2). Trust sales proceeds do not include amounts paid for any interest income that would be required to be reported under § 1.6045-1(d)(3). Trust sales proceeds also do not include amounts paid to a NMWHFIT as the result of pro-rata sales of trust assets to effect a redemption described in paragraph (c)(2)(iv)(G) of this section or the value of assets received as a result of a tax-free corporate reorganization as described in paragraph (c)(2)(iv)(H) of this section.

* * * * *

(c) * * *

(2) * * *

(ii) * * *

(A) All items of gross income (including OID, except that OID is not required to be included for a WHMT that has a start-up date (as defined in paragraph (b)(19) of this section) prior to August 13, 1998).

* * * * *

(iv) Asset sales and dispositions. The trustee must report information regarding sales and dispositions of WHFIT assets as required in this paragraph (c)(2)(iv). For purposes of this paragraph (c)(2)(iv), a payment (other than a final scheduled payment) that completely retires a debt instrument (including a mortgage held by a WHMT) or a pro-rata prepayment on a debt instrument (see § 1.1275-2(f)(2)) held by a WHFIT must be reported as a full or partial sale or disposition of the debt instrument. Pro-rata sales of trust assets to effect redemptions, as defined in paragraph (c)(2)(iv)(G) of this section, or exchanges of trust assets as the result of a corporate reorganization under paragraph (c)(2)(iv)(H) of this section, are not reported as sales or dispositions under this paragraph (c)(2)(iv).

(A) General rule. Except as provided in paragraph (c)(2)(iv)(B) (regarding the exception for certain NMWHFITs) or paragraph (c)(2)(iv)(C) (regarding the exception for certain WHMTs) of this section, the trustee must report with respect to each sale or disposition of a WHFIT asset—

(1) The date of each sale or disposition;

(2) Information that enables a requesting person to determine the amount of trust sales proceeds (as defined in paragraph (b)(21) of this section) attributable to a beneficial owner as a result of each sale or disposition; and

(3) Information that enables a beneficial owner to allocate, with reasonable accuracy, a portion of the owner's basis in its trust interest to each sale or disposition.

(B) Exception for certain NMWHFITs. If a NMWHFIT meets paragraph (c)(2)(iv)(D)(1)(regarding the general de minimis test), paragraph (c)(2)(iv)(E) (regarding the qualified NMWHFIT exception), or paragraph (c)(2)(iv)(F) (regarding the NMWHFIT final calendar year exception) of this section, the trustee is not required to report under paragraph (c)(2)(iv)(A) of this section. Instead, the trustee must report sufficient information to enable a requesting person to determine the amount of trust sales proceeds distributed to a beneficial owner during the calendar year with respect to each sale or disposition of a trust asset. The trustee also must provide requesting persons with a statement that the NMWHFIT is permitted to report under this paragraph (c)(2)(iv)(B).

(C) Exception for certain WHMTs. If a WHMT meets either the general or the special de minimis test of paragraph (c)(2)(iv)(D) of this section for the calendar year, the trustee is not required to report under paragraph (c)(2)(iv)(A) of this section. Instead, the trustee must report information to enable a requesting person to determine the amount of trust sales proceeds attributable to a beneficial owner as a result of the sale or disposition. The trustee also must provide requesting persons with a statement that the WHMT is permitted to report under this paragraph (c)(2)(iv)(C).

(D) De minimis tests—(1) General WHFIT de minimis test. The general WHFIT de minimis test is satisfied if trust sales proceeds for the calendar year are not more than five percent of the net asset value of the trust (aggregate fair market value of the trust's assets less the trust's liabilities) as of the later of January 1 and the start-up date (as defined paragraph (b)(19) of this section); or, if the trustee chooses, the later of January 1 and the measuring date. The measuring date is the date of the last deposit of assets into the WHFIT (not including any deposit of assets into the WHFIT pursuant to a distribution reinvestment program), not to exceed 90 days after the date the registration statement of the WHFIT becomes effective under the Securities Act of 1933.

(2) Special WHMT de minimis test. A WHMT that meets the asset requirement of paragraph (g)(1)(ii)(E) of this section satisfies the special WHMT de minimis test in this paragraph (c)(2)(iv)(D)(2) if trust sales proceeds for the calendar year are not more than five percent of the aggregate outstanding principal balance of the WHMT (as defined in paragraph (g)(1)(iii)(D) of this section) as of the later of January 1 of that year or the trust's start-up date. For purposes of applying the special WHMT de minimis test in this paragraph (c)(2)(iv)(D)(2), amounts that result from the complete or partial payment of the outstanding principal balance of the mortgages held by the trust are not included in the amount of trust sales proceeds. The IRS and the Treasury Department may provide by revenue ruling, or by other published guidance, that the special de minimis test of this paragraph (c)(2)(iv)(D)(2) may be applied to WHFITs holding debt instruments other

than those described in paragraph (g)(1)(ii)(E) of this section.

(3) Effect of clean-up call. If a WHFIT fails to meet either de minimis test described in this paragraph (c)(2)(iv)(D) solely as the result of a clean-up call, as defined in paragraph (b)(6) of this section, the WHFIT will be treated as having met the de minimis test.

(4) Exception for certain fully reported sales—(i) Rule. If a trustee of a NMWHFIT reports the sales described in paragraph (c)(2)(iv)(D)(4)(ii) of this section as provided under paragraph (c)(2)(iv)(A) of this section (regardless of whether the general minimis test in paragraph (c)(2)(iv)(D)(1) of this section is satisfied for a particular calendar year) consistently throughout the life of the WHFIT, a trustee may exclude the trust sales proceeds received by the WHFIT as a result of those sales from the trust sales proceeds used to determine whether a WHFIT has satisfied the general de minimis test in paragraph (c)(2)(iv)(D)(1) of this section.

(ii) Applicable sales and dispositions. This paragraph (c)(2)(iv)(D)(4) applies to sales and dispositions resulting from corporate reorganizations and restructurings for which the trust receives cash, the sale of assets received by the trust in corporate reorganizations and restructurings (including conversions of closed-end investment companies to open-end investment companies), principal prepayments, bond calls, bond maturities, and the sale of securities by the trustee as required by the governing document or applicable law governing fiduciaries in order to maintain the sound investment character of the trust, and any other nonvolitional dispositions of trust assets.

(iii) Certain small sales and dispositions. If the amount of trust sales proceeds from a sale or disposition described in paragraph (c)(2)(iv)(D)(4)(ii) of this section is less than .01 percent of the net fair market value of the WHFIT as determined for applying the de minimis test for the calendar year, the trustee is not required to report the sale or disposition under paragraph (c)(2)(iv)(A) of this section provided the trustee includes the trust sales proceeds, received for purposes of determining whether the trust has met the general de minimis test of paragraph (c)(2)(iv)(D)(1) of this section.

(E) Qualified NMWHFIT exception. The qualified NMWHFIT exception is satisfied if—

(1) The NMWHFIT has a start-up date (as defined in paragraph (b)(19) of this section) before February 23, 2006;

(2) The registration statement of the NMWHFIT becomes effective under the Securities Act of 1933, as amended (15 U.S.C. 77a, et seq.) and trust interests are offered for sale to the public before February 23, 2006; or

(3) The registration statement of the NMWHFIT becomes effective under the Securities Act of 1933 and trust interests are offered for sale to the public on or after February 23, 2006, and before July 31, 2006, and the NMWHFIT is fully funded before October 1, 2006. For purposes of determining whether a NMWHFIT is fully funded under this paragraph (c)(2)(iv)(E), deposits to the NMWHFIT after October 1, 2006, that are made pursuant to a distribution reinvestment program that is consistent with the requirements of § 301.7701-4(c) of this chapter are disregarded.

(F) NMWHFIT final calendar year exception. The NMWHFIT final calendar year exception is satisfied if—

(1) The NMWHFIT terminates on or before December 31 of the year for which the trustee is reporting;

(2) Beneficial owners exchange their interests for cash or are treated as having exchanged their interests for cash upon termination of the trust; and

(3) The trustee makes reasonable efforts to engage in pro-rata sales of trust assets to effect redemptions.

(G) Pro-rata sales of trust assets to effect a redemption—(1) Rule. Pro-rata sales of trust assets to effect redemptions are not required to be reported under this paragraph (c)(2)(iv).

(2) Definition. Pro-rata sales of trust assets to effect redemptions occur when—

(i) One or more trust interests are tendered for redemption;

(ii) The trustee identifies the pro-rata shares of the trust assets that are deemed to be owned by the trust interest or interests tendered for redemption (See paragraph (b)(8) of this section for a description of how pro-rata is to be applied for purposes of this paragraph (c)(2)(iv)(G)) and sells those assets as soon as practicable;

(iii) Proceeds from the sales of the assets identified in paragraph (c)(2)(iv)(G)(2)(ii) of this section are used solely to effect redemptions; and

(iv) The redemptions are reported as required under paragraph (c)(2)(v) of this section by the trustee.

(3) Additional rules—(i) Calendar month aggregation. The trustee may compare the aggregate pro-rata share of the assets deemed to be owned by the trust interests tendered for redemption during the calendar month with the aggregate sales of assets to effect redemptions for the calendar month to determine the pro-rata sales of trust assets to effect redemptions for the calendar month. If the aggregate pro-rata share of an asset deemed to be owned by the trust interests tendered for redemption for the month is a fractional amount, the trustee may round that number up to the next whole number for the purpose of determining the pro-rata sales to effect redemptions for the calendar month;

(ii) Sales of assets to effect redemptions may be combined with sales of assets for other purposes. Sales of assets to effect redemptions may be combined with the sales of assets to obtain cash for other purposes but the proceeds from the sales of assets to effect redemptions must be used solely to provide cash for redemptions and the sales of assets to obtain cash for other purposes must be reported as otherwise provided in this paragraph (c)(2)(iv). For example, if a trustee sells assets and the proceeds are used by the trustee to pay trust expenses, these amounts are to be included in the amounts reported under paragraph (c)(2)(iv)(A) or (B), as appropriate.

(4) Example—(i) January 1, 2008. Trust has one million trust interests and all interests have equal value and equal rights. The number of shares of stock in corporations A through J and the pro-rata share of each stock that a trust interest is deemed to own as of January 1, 2008, is as follows:

Stock	Total shares	Per trust interest
A	24,845	.024845
B	28,273	.028273
C	35,575	.035575
D	13,866	.013866
E	25,082	.025082
F	39,154	.039154
G	16,137	.016137
H	14,704	.014704
I	17,436	.017436
J	31,133	.031133

(ii) Transactions of January 2, 2008. On January 2, 2008, 50,000 trust interests are tendered for redemption. The deemed pro-rata ownership of stocks A through J represented by the 50,000 redeemed trust interests and the stocks sold to provide cash for the redemptions are set out in the following table:

Stock	Deemed pro-rata ownership	Shares sold
A	1,242.25	1,242
B	1,413.65	1,413
C	1,778.75	1,779
D	693.30	694
E	1,254.10	1,254
F	1,957.70	1,957
G	806.85	807
H	735.20	735
I	871.80	872
J	1,556.65	1,557

(iii) Transactions on January 15 through 17, 2008. On January 15, 2008, 10,000 trust interests are tendered for redemption. Trustee lends money to Trust for redemptions. On January 16, B merges into C at a rate of .55 per share. On January 17, Trustee sells stock to obtain cash to be reimbursed the cash loaned to Trust to effect the redemptions. The pro-rata share of the stock deemed to be owned by the 10,000 redeemed trust interests and the stock sold by the trustee to effect the redemptions are set out in the following table:

| Stock | Deemed pro-rata ownership | Shares sold |
| A | 248.45 | 249 |

B	00	00
C	511.25	512
D	138.66	138
E	250.82	251
F	391.54	392
G	161.37	162
H	147.04	148
I	174.36	174
J	311.33	311

(iv) Transactions on January 28 and 29, 2008. On January 28, 2008, the value of the H stock is $30.00 per share and Trustee, pursuant to Trust's governing document, sells the H stock to preserve the financial integrity of Trust and receives $414,630. Trustee intends to report this sale under paragraph (c)(2)(iv)(A) of this section and to distribute the proceeds of the sale pro-rata to trust interest holders on Trust's next scheduled distribution date. On January 29, 2008, while trustee still holds the proceeds from the January 28 sale, 10,000 trust interests are tendered for redemption. The pro-rata share of the stock deemed to be owned by the 10,000 redeemed trust interests and the stock sold by the trustee to effect the redemptions are set out in the following table:

Stock	Deemed pro-rata ownership	Shares sold
A	248.45	248
B	0	0
C	511.25	511
D	138.66	139
E	250.82	251
F	391.54	391
G	161.37	161
H	10	0
I	174.36	175
J	311.33	312

(v) Monthly amounts. To determine the pro-rata sales to effect redemptions for January, trustee compares the aggregate pro-rata share of stocks A through J (rounded to the next whole number) deemed to be owned by the trust interests tendered for redemption during the month of January with the sales of stocks A through J to effect redemptions:

Stock	Deemed pro-rata ownership	Shares sold
A	1740	1739
B	0	0
C	3579	3579
D	971	971
E	1756	1756
F	2741	2741
G	1130	1130
H	883	883

(vi) Pro-rata sales to effect redemptions for the month of January. For the month of January, the deemed pro-rata ownership of shares of stocks A through J equal or exceed the sales of stock to effect redemptions for the month. Accordingly, all of the sales to effect redemptions during the month of January are considered to be pro-rata and are not required to be reported under this paragraph (c)(2)(iv).

(H) Corporate Reorganizations. The exchange of trust assets for other assets of equivalent value pursuant to a tax free corporate reorganization is not required to be reported as a sale or disposition under this paragraph (c)(2)(iv).

(v) Redemptions and sales of WHFIT interests—(A) Redemptions—(1) In general. Unless paragraph (c)(2)(v)(C) of this section applies, for each date on which the amount of a redemption proceeds for the redemption of a trust interest is determined, the trustee must provide information to enable a requesting person to determine—

(i) The redemption proceeds (as defined in paragraph (b)(15) of this section) per trust interest on that date;

(ii) The redemption asset proceeds (as defined in paragraph (b)(14) of this section) per trust interest on that date; and

(iii) The gross income that is attributable to the redeeming beneficial owner for the portion of the calendar year that the redeeming beneficial owner held its interest (including income earned by the WHFIT after the date of the last income distribution.

(2) In kind redemptions. The value of the assets received with respect to an in-kind redemption (as defined in paragraph (b)(8) of this section) is not required to be reported under this paragraph (c)(2)(v)(A). Information regarding the income attributable to a redeeming beneficial owner must, however, be reported under paragraph (c)(2)(v)(A)(1)(iii) of this section.

(B) Sale of a trust interest. Under paragraph (c)(2)(v)(C) of this section applies, if a secondary market for interests in the WHFIT is established, the trustee must provide, for each day of the calendar year, information to enable requesting persons to determine—

(1) The sale assets proceeds (as defined in paragraph (b)(17) of this section) per trust interest on that date; and

(2) The gross income that is attributable to a selling beneficial owner and to a purchasing beneficial owner for the portion of the calendar year that each held the trust interest.

(C) Simplified Reporting for Certain NMWHFITs—(1) In general. The trustee of an NMWHFIT described in paragraph (c)(2)(v)(C)(2) of this section is not required to report the information described in paragraph (c)(2)(v)(A) of this section (regarding redemptions) or (c)(2)(v)(B) of this section (regarding sales). However, the trustee must report to requesting persons, for each date on which the amount of redemption proceeds to be paid for the redemption of a trust interest is determined, information that will enable requesting persons to determine the redemption proceeds per trust interest on that date. The trustee also must provide requesting persons with a statement that this paragraph applies to the NMWHFIT.

(2) NMWHFITs that qualify for the exception. This paragraph (c)(2)(v)(C) applies to a NMWHFIT if—

(i) Substantially all the assets of the NMWHFIT produce income that is treated as interest income (but only if these assets trade on a recognized exchange or securities market without a price component attributable to accrued interest) or produce dividend income (as defined in section 6042(b) and the regulations under that section). (Trust sales proceeds and gross proceeds from sales described in paragraphs (c)(2)(iv)(G) and (H) of this section are ignored for the purpose of determining if substantially all of a NMWHFIT's assets produce dividend or the interest income described in this paragraph); and

(ii) The qualified NMWHFIT exception of paragraph (c)(2)(iv)(E) of this section is satisfied, or the trustee is required by the governing document of the NMWHFIT to determine and distribute all cash held for distribution (as defined in paragraph (b)(5) of this section) no less frequently than monthly. A NMWHFIT will be considered to have satisfied this paragraph (c)(2)(v)(C)(2)(i) notwithstanding that the governing document of the NMWHFIT permits the trustee to forego making a required monthly or more frequent distribution, if the cash held for distribution is less than 0.1 percent of the aggregate net asset value of the trust as of the date specified in the governing document for calculating the amount of the monthly distribution.

(vi) Information regarding bond premium. The trustee generally must report information that enables a beneficial owner to determine, in any manner that is reasonably consistent with section 171, the amount of the beneficial owner's amortizable bond premium, if any, for each calendar year. However, if a NMWHFIT meets the general de minimis test in paragraph (c)(2)(iv)(D)(1) of this section, the qualified NMWHFIT exception of paragraph (c)(2)(iv)(E) of this section, or the NMWHFIT final calendar year exception of paragraph (c)(2)(iv)(F) of this section, the trustee of the NMWHFIT is not required to report information regarding bond premium.

(vii) Information regarding market discount. The trustee generally must report information that enables a beneficial owner to determine, in any manner reasonably consistent with section 1276 (including section 1276(a)(3)), the amount of market discount that has accrued during the calendar year. However, if a NMWHFIT meets the general de minimis test in paragraph (c)(2)(iv)(D) of this section, the qualified NMWHFIT exception of paragraph (c)(2)(iv)(E) of this section, or the NMWHFIT final calendar year exception of paragraph (c)(2)(iv)(F) of this section, the trustee of such NMWHFIT is not required to provide information regarding market discount.

* * * * *

(d) * * *

(2) * * *

(ii) * * *

(C) Gross income. All items of gross income of the WHFIT attributable to the TIH for the calendar year (including OID (unless the exception for certain WHMTs applies (see paragraph (c)(2)(ii)(A) of this section)) and all amounts of income attributable to a selling, purchasing, or redeeming TIH for the portion of the calendar year that the TIH held its interest (unless paragraph (c)(2)(v)(C) of this section (regarding an exception for certain NMWHFITs) applies));

* * * * *

(F) Reporting Redemptions. All redemption asset proceeds (as defined in paragraph (b)(14) of this section) paid to the TIH for the calendar year, if any, or, if paragraph (c)(2)(v)(C) of this section (regarding an exception for certain NMWHFITs) applies, all redemption proceeds (as defined in paragraph (b)(15) of this section) paid to the TIH for the calendar year;

(G) Reporting sales of a trust interest on a secondary market. All sales asset proceeds (as defined in paragraph (b)(17) of this section) paid to the TIH for the sale of a trust interest or interests on a secondary market established for the NMWHFIT for the calendar year, if any, or, if paragraph (c)(2)(v)(C) of this section (regarding an exception for certain NMWHFITs) applies, all sales proceeds (as defined in paragraph (b)(18) of this section) paid to the TIH for the calendar year; and

* * * * *

(f) Safe harbor for providing information for certain NMWHFITs—(1) Safe harbor for trustee reporting of NMWHFIT information. The trustee of a NMWHFIT that meets the requirements of paragraph (f)(1)(i) of this section is deemed to satisfy paragraph (c)(1)(i) of this section, if the trustee calculates and provides WHFIT information in the manner described in this paragraph (f) and provides a statement to a requesting person giving notice that information has been calculated in accordance with this paragraph (f)(1).

(i) In general—(A) Eligibility to report under this safe harbor. Only NMWHFITs that meet the requirements set forth in paragraphs (f)(1)(i)(A)(1) and (2) of this section may report under this safe harbor. For purposes of determining whether the requirements of paragraph (f)(1)(i)(A)(1) of this section are met, trust sales proceeds and gross proceeds from sales described in paragraphs (c)(2)(iv)(G) and (H) of this section are ignored.

(1) Substantially all of the NMWHFIT's income is from dividends or interest; and

(2) All trust interests have identical value and rights.

* * * * *

(viii) Reporting market discount information under the safe harbor—(A) In general— (1) Trustee required to provide market discount information. If the trustee is required to provide information regarding market discount under paragraph (c)(2)(vii) of this section, the trustee must provide—

(i) The information required to be provided under paragraph (f)(1)(iv)(A)(1)(iii) of this section; and

(ii) If the NMWHFIT holds debt instruments with OID, a list of the aggregate adjusted issue prices of the debt instruments per trust interest calculated as of the start-up date or measuring date (see paragraph (c)(2)(iv)(D)(4) of this section) (whichever provides more accurate information) and as of January 1 for each subsequent year of the NMWHFIT.

(2) Trustee not required to provide market discount information. If the trustee is not required to provide market discount information under paragraph (c)(2)(vii) of this section (because the NMWHFIT meets the general de minimis test of paragraph (c)(2)(iv)(D)(1) of this section, the qualified NMWHFIT exception of paragraph (c)(2)(iv)(E) of this section, or the NMWHFIT final year exception of paragraph (c)(2)(iv)(F) of this section), the trustee is not required under this paragraph (f) to provide any information regarding market discount.

* * * * *

(2) * * *

(viii) * * *

(A) Except as provided in paragraph (f)(2)(viii)(B) of this section, the trustee or middleman must provide the TIH with the information provided under paragraph (f)(1)(viii) of this section.

(3) * * *

(i) * * *

(A) * * *

(1) Trust is a NMWHFIT that holds common stock in ten different corporations and has 100 trust interests outstanding. The start-up date for Trust is December 15, 2006, and Trust's registration statement under the Securities Act of 1933 became effective after July 31, 2006. Trust terminates on March 15, 2008. The agreement governing Trust requires Trust to distribute cash held by Trust reduced by accrued but unpaid expenses on April 15, July 15, and October 15 of the 2007 calendar year. The agreement also provides that the trust interests will be redeemed by the Trust for an amount equal to the value of the trust interest, as of the close of business, on the day the trust interest is tendered for redemption. There is no reinvestment plan. A secondary market for interests in Trust will

be created by Trust's sponsor and Trust's sponsor will provide Trustee with a list of dates on which sales occurred on this secondary market.

(B) * * *

(5) On June 1, 2007, Trustee sells shares of stock for $1000x to preserve the soundness of the trust. The stock sold on June 1, 2007, equaled 20% of the aggregate fair market value of the assets held by Trust on the start-up date of Trust. Trustee has chosen not to report sales described in paragraph (c)(2)(iv)(4)(ii) of Trust's assets under paragraph (c)(2)(iv)(D)(4) of this section.

* * * * *

(9) On December 10, 2007, J tenders a trust interest to Trustee for redemption through Broker1. Trustee determines that the amount of the redemption proceeds to be paid for a trust interest that is tendered for redemption on December 10, 2007 is $116x, of which $115x represents the redemption asset proceeds. Trustee pays this amount to Broker1 on J's behalf. On December 12, 2007, trustee engages in a non pro-rata sale of shares of common stock for $115x to effect J's redemption of a trust interest. The stock sold on December 12, 2007, equals 2% of the aggregate fair market value of all the assets of Trust as of the start-up date.

* * * * *

(ii) * * *

(B) * * *

(4) * * * (i) Application of the de minimis test. The aggregate fair market value of the assets of Trust as of January 1, 2007, was $10,000x. During the 2007 calendar year, Trust received trust sales proceeds of $1115x. The trust sales proceeds received by Trust for the 2007 calendar year equal 11.15% of Trust's fair market value as of January 1, 2007. Accordingly, the de minimis test is not satisfied for the 2007 calendar year. The qualified NMWHFIT exception in paragraph (c)(2)(iv)(E) of this section and the NMWHFIT final calendar year exception in (c)(2)(iv)(F) of this section also do not apply to Trust for the 2007 calendar year.

* * * * *

(5) Reporting redemptions. Because Trust is not required to make distributions at least as frequently as monthly, and Trust does not satisfy the qualified NMWHFIT exception in paragraph (c)(2)(iv)(E) of this section, the exception in paragraph (c)(2)(v)(C) does not apply to Trust. To satisfy the requirements of paragraph (f)(1) of this section, Trustee provides a list of dates for which the redemption proceeds to be paid for the redemption of a trust interest was determined for the 2007 calendar year and the redemptions asset proceeds paid for each date. During 2007, Trustee only determined the amount of redemption proceeds paid for the redemption of a trust interest once, for December 10, 2007 and the redemption asset proceeds determined for that date was $115x.

(6) Reporting sales of trust interests. Because trust is not required to make distributions at least as frequently as monthly, and Trust does not satisfy the qualified NMWHFIT exception in paragraph (c)(2)(iv)(E) of this section, the exception in paragraph (c)(2)(v)(C) of this section does not apply to Trust. Sponsor, in accordance with the trust agreement, provides Trustee with a list of dates on which sales on the secondary market occurred. To satisfy the requirements of paragraph (f)(1) of this section, Trustee provides requesting persons with a list of dates on which sales on the secondary market occurred and the amount of cash held for distribution, per trust interest, on each date. The first sale during the 2007 calendar year occurred on September 30, 2007, and the amount of cash held for distribution, per trust interest, on that date is $1.35x. The second sale occurred on December 10, 2007, and the amount of cash held for distribution, per trust interest, on that date is $1.00x.

(g) * * *

(1) * * *

(iv) * * * (A) * * *

(2) In calculating the daily portion of OID, the trustee must use the prepayment assumption used in pricing the original issue of trust interests. If the WHMT has a start-up date prior to January 24, 2006, and the trustee, after a good faith effort to ascertain that information, does not know the prepayment assumption used in pricing the original issue of trust interests, the trustee may use any reasonable prepayment assumption to calculate OID provided it continues to use the same prepayment assumption consistently thereafter.

* * * * *

(v) * * * (A) * * *

(3) Computing the total amount of stated interest remaining to be paid and the total remaining OID at the beginning of the month. To compute the total amount of stated interest remaining to be paid to the WHMT as of the beginning of the month and the total remaining OID as of the beginning of the month, the trustee must use the prepayment assumption used in pricing the original issue of trust interests. If the WHMT has a start-up date prior to January 24, 2006, and the trustee, after a good faith effort to ascertain that information, does not know the prepayment assumption used in pricing the original issue of trust interests, the trustee may use any reasonable prepayment assumption to calculate these amounts provided it continues to use the same prepayment assumption consistently thereafter.

* * * * *

(h) Additional safe harbors—(1) Temporary safe harbor for WHMTs—(i) Application. Pending the issuance of additional guidance, the safe harbor in this paragraph applies to trustees and middlemen of WHMTs that are not eligible to report under the WHMT safe harbor in paragraph (g) of this section because they hold interests in another WHFIT, in a

REMIC, or hold or issue stripped interests.

(ii) Safe harbor. A trustee is deemed to satisfy the requirements of paragraph (c) of this section, if the trustee calculates and provides trust information in a manner that enables a requesting person to provide trust information to a beneficial owner of a trust interest that enables the owner to reasonably accurately report the tax consequences of its ownership of a trust interest on its federal income tax return. Additionally, to be deemed to satisfy the requirements of paragraph (c) of this section, the trustee must calculate and provide trust information regarding market discount and OID by any reasonable manner consistent with section 1272(a)(6). A middleman or a trustee may satisfy its obligation to furnish information to the IRS under paragraph (d) of this section and to the trust interest holder under paragraph (e) of this section by providing information consistent with the information provided under this paragraph by the trustee.

(2) Additional safe harbors provided by other published guidance. The IRS and the Treasury Department may provide additional safe harbor reporting procedures for complying with this section or a specific paragraph of this section by other published guidance (see § 601.601(d)(2) of this chapter).

* * * * *

(m) Penalties for failure to comply—(1) In general. Every trustee or middleman who fails to comply with the reporting obligations imposed by this section is subject to penalties under sections 6721, 6722, and any other applicable penalty provisions.

(2) Penalties not imposed on trustees and middlemen of certain WHMTs for failure to report OID. Penalties will not be imposed as a result of a failure to provide OID information for a WHMT that has a start-up date on or after August 13, 1998 and on or before January 24, 2006, if the trustee of the WHMT does not have the historic information necessary to provide this information and the trustee demonstrates that it has attempted in good faith, but without success, to obtain this information. For purposes of calculating a market discount fraction under paragraph (g)(1)(v) of this section, for a WHMT described in this paragraph, it may be assumed that the WHMT is holding mortgages that were issued without OID. A trustee availing itself of this paragraph must include a statement to that effect when providing information to requesting persons under paragraph (c) of these regulations.

* * * * *

§ 1.671-5T [Removed]

Par. 3. Section 1.671-5T is removed.

Kevin M. Brown,

Deputy Commissioner for Services and Enforcement.
Eric Solomon,
Assistant Secretary (Tax Policy).
[FR Doc. 06-9924 Filed 12-26-06; 10:22 am]
BILLING CODE 4830-01-P

Made in the USA
Columbia, SC
07 February 2022